IT'S A FACT!

Real-Life Reads

DESERT SURVIVAL HANDBOOK

by Ruth Owen

Consultant:

Suzy Gazlay, MA
Recipient, Presidential Award for Excellence in Science Teaching

Ruby Tuesday Books

Published in 2014 by Ruby Tuesday Books Ltd.

Editor: Mark J. Sachner
Designer: Emma Randall
Production: John Lingham

Photo Credits:
Alamy: 20–21; Istock: 22–23, 31; Shutterstock: Cover, 4–5, 6–7, 8–9,
10–11, 12–13, 14–15, 16–17, 18–19, 23, 24–25, 26–27, 28, 31.

Library of Congress Control Number: 2013920127

ISBN 978-1-909673-56-4

Printed and published in the United States of America

For further information including rights and permissions requests, please
contact our Customer Service Department at 877-337-8577.

CONTENTS

Survive or Die?

The day began well. You were excited about hiking in the desert. Then you accidentally wandered off the hiking **trail**.

Now you are lost. You have walked for hours, hoping to find another trail or road. But all you see in every direction is dry, rocky land.

Your water bottle is nearly empty. You have no food, no tent, and your cell phone is dead. Your only hope is to use your desert survival skills.

Will you survive or die?

An Extreme Environment

A desert is one of the toughest **environments** on Earth for a human to face. Some deserts are hot, while others are cold.

A desert is a place that receives less than 10 inches (25 cm) of rain or snow each year. Some deserts receive no rain or snow for months or even years at a time.

During a summer day, the temperature in a hot desert might rise to 140°F (60°C). The extreme heat and lack of water makes survival in this hot, dry environment very difficult.

The Sun's rays reflect off the ground and rocks, pumping more heat into the air.

The glare of the Sun will hurt your eyes.

Countdown

From the moment you get lost in a desert, you are in a life-or-death countdown.

Finding water to drink must become your number one priority. Without water, your body will stop working properly, day by day.

DAY 1

Headaches

Muscle cramps

DAY 2

Extreme thirst

Dizziness

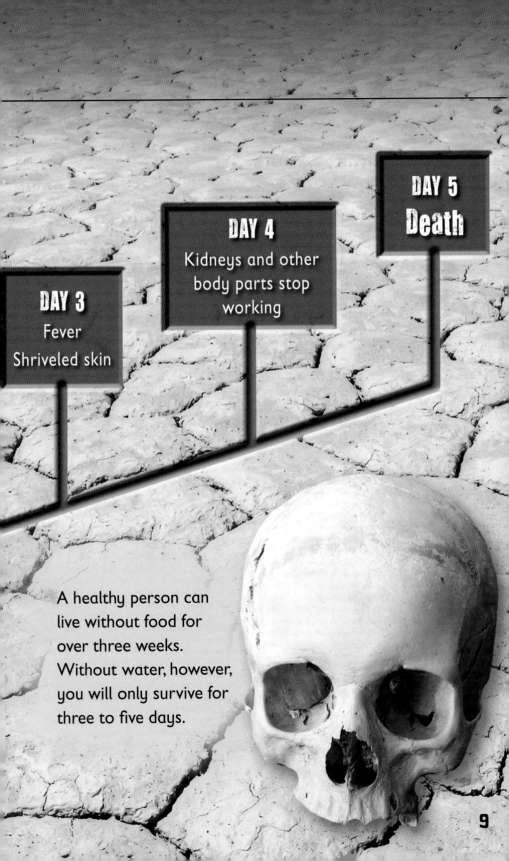

DAY 3
Fever
Shriveled skin

DAY 4
Kidneys and other
body parts stop
working

DAY 5
Death

A healthy person can
live without food for
over three weeks.
Without water, however,
you will only survive for
three to five days.

Desert Water Secrets

Finding water in a desert might seem impossible, but it can be done.

If it does rain in a desert, rainwater may collect in dips and cracks in rocks. Bird droppings on a rock can be a clue that birds have been visiting that place to drink. Push a piece of cloth into the crack to soak up the water. Then wring out the liquid into your mouth.

Dips and cracks in rocks can hold water.

Droppings show that birds visit a spot.

Dew

Dew will settle on rocks and grass overnight. Before the Sun rises and dries the dew, soak it up with a cloth. Then suck the dew from the cloth.

A barrel cactus

Stem

A barrel cactus can store gallons of water inside its fat stems. Cut open the plant to reach the water-filled flesh inside. The flesh will taste bitter and soapy. All you need to do, however, is take a bite, suck out the liquid, and then spit out the flesh.

Save Your Body's Water

Finding water is a priority in a desert.
So is stopping your body from losing water.

Sweating is one way that your body keeps from overheating. Sweat cools your skin, and as it **evaporates** into the air, it takes a little of your body's heat away with it. In a hot desert, however, your body can sweat out 2 pints (1 liter) of water every hour!

To avoid sweating, try to find some shade. Cover your head and do not take off your clothes. Your clothing will soak up your sweat. Then the wet clothes will help cool you. Walk or do activities only at night, when it's much cooler.

Precious Water

Hot desert. No water. What have some survival experts done to get a drink? They have actually drunk their own pee!

Pee, or urine, is a mixture of waste products and water. Pee that looks sludgy, or a dark yellow or brownish color, contains more waste than water. This is not safe to drink. If pee is a clear, pale yellow color, however, it means it is mostly water. This precious liquid can be collected in a bottle for drinking.

And what does pee taste like? It tastes nasty, of course. But in a survival situation, a person can't afford to waste water!

Finding Shelter

After the search for water, finding or building a shelter is your next priority.

Even the hottest deserts can be very cold at night. So a shelter gives you warmth at night and cooling shade by day. Having a place to "call home" will also give you comfort.

Cliffs, rock piles, or large bushes can offer shade and protection. It may also be possible to dig an underground shelter. Only work in the early morning or just before dark, when it's cooler.

1: Find a natural dip or trench in the ground, or dig one with a sharp rock, a branch, or your hands.

Trench

2: If you have a blanket or other sheet of material (see page 26) lay it over the trench. Hold it in place with rocks and sand.

You could also use branches from bushes to cover the trench.

Rocks

Blanket

Building a Fire

If you are in a desert where there are plants, you can find fuel to build a fire.

A fire will keep you warm at night and keep you from feeling so alone. A fire will also frighten away animals such as coyotes or wild dogs.

If you have no matches, use the Sun to light your fire. A pair of glasses or even water in a plastic bottle will focus the Sun's rays onto dry grass until it catches fire.

Collect fuel such as dead branches, bark, and dry grass during cool parts of the day.

Desert Food Supplies

Your stomach may be growling, but it's possible to live for weeks without food.

Also, your body uses up water as it digests food. So if you've not drunk much water, it's better not to eat.

A honeypot ant

Some ants taste sweet because they store honey in their bodies. They make the honey from desert plants.

Once you have a water supply, however, food can be found in a desert. One type of food that some survival experts eat is insects. Ants, termites, and insect **larvae**, or grubs, contain more **protein** than steak. Insects can be eaten raw or boiled in water to make a bug soup!

This Australian witchetty grub is the larva of a moth. It tastes like almonds.

Witchetty grub

Honey inside the ant's body

Trapped in a Sandstorm

Scorching heat and lack of water are not the only dangers in a desert.

In the distance, you see the vast cloud of sand approaching. It's traveling toward you at 100 miles an hour (160 km/h). Within seconds, you are trapped in a **sandstorm**. The thick, whirling sand feels like someone rubbing sandpaper on your skin.

Sit or lie down and cover your head with your arms. A sandstorm may last for minutes, hours, or even days. All you can do is wait.

Cover your face to keep the thick sand from filling your nose and mouth and choking you.

Keep your eyes tightly closed—even if you're wearing glasses.

Never Give Up

If you are lost in a desert, don't panic. Find water, find shelter, try not to move around too much, and wait to be rescued.

Keeping a fire burning will help rescuers in planes spot you. Any time you leave your shelter, draw a large arrow in the sand to show rescuers the direction you took.

Use rocks to make a large V on the ground. Pilots around the world know that V means "help is needed." If a pilot spots your sign, he or she will rock the plane's wings from side to side. Then you will know that help is on the way.

Desert Survival Fact File

Be Prepared

If you plan to spend time in a desert environment, carry survival equipment and be prepared.

- Go to a training class to learn survival skills.
- Tell someone where you are going and how long you will be gone.
- Hike with a buddy—don't hike alone.
- Carry a cell phone and a spare battery.
- You need to drink some water every hour if it is hot, so carry plenty of water!

Survival Equipment

- A pocket knife

- Matches in a waterproof container

- A compass to show if you are heading north, east, south, or west

- A space blanket that can be used to make a shelter

- A large, plastic trash bag that folds up to be tiny, and can be used for carrying water or as a covering for your body

- A tin cup for cooking over a fire

So You're Lost—What's Next?

If you do get lost, try not to panic. Think **STOP**:

S = Sit down and take deep breaths.
T = Think calmly about your situation. What do you need?
What equipment do you have?
O = Observe the area around you. For example, is there a place
where you can find shelter?
P = Prepare for survival by collecting water, finding shelter, and
gathering fuel for a fire.

Make a survival pattern that puts your tasks
in order of priority:

1: Water
2: Shelter
3: Fire
4: Food

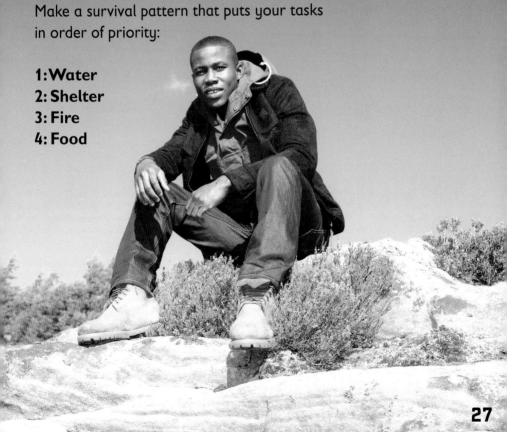

Desert Survival Fact File

Water Tips

- Keep checking the sky for clouds, as storms can blow up fast. Be ready to collect as much rain as possible, using any container or waterproof item you have.
- Look for dried-up streams, rivers, or water holes. Dig down into the ground, as there may still be water under the surface.

Dried-up stream

Your Emergency Home

- Decide on a place to be your home base. Having a base to return to after trips to find water or fuel will give you comfort.
- A shelter doesn't have to be large. It only needs to be big enough to protect your body.
- Only build a small fire so it will need less fuel to keep it burning.

Food Tips

- Some plants, especially their berries, may be poisonous to eat. Don't risk it. It's better to be hungry than sick.

DO NOT EAT:

- Any insect that has a strong smell
- Mosquitoes or flies that can carry disease
- Colorful insects • Hairy insects • Spiders

Staying Safe

- It's hard to estimate distance in an empty desert. Something that looks about 1 mile (1.6 km) away could actually be 3 miles (4.8 km) away. So plan trips away from your base carefully.

Deserts are home to scorpions, snakes, and other animals that sting or bite.

- Watch where you walk, and never put your feet or hands somewhere you cannot see.
- When picking up rocks or branches, be alert. Snakes or scorpions may be taking shelter beneath them.
- Carefully check the ground before you sit or lie down.
- Check inside shoes and shake out clothes before putting them on.
- Check a sleeping bag or shelter before climbing inside.

Scorpion

Glossary

dew (DOO)
Water that collects on grass and other objects close to the ground. Dew forms when air cools down at night. This causes water vapor in the air to cool, too, and turn into liquid water. Dew can usually be seen in the early morning.

environment (en-VIE-ruhn-ment)
The air, land, rivers, lakes, plants, soil, and everything in an area. An environment can be a natural one, such as a desert, or be made by humans, such as a city.

evaporate (ee-VAP-uh-rate)
To turn from liquid water into a gas called water vapor that floats in the air.

larva (LAR-vuh)
A young insect that looks like a fat worm. Many insects have four life stages, which are egg, larva, pupa, and adult.

protein (PROH-teen)
A substance needed by humans and other animals for health and growth. Foods that contain protein include meat, fish, eggs, and nuts.

sandstorm (SAND-storm)
A huge, fast-moving cloud of sand. Sandstorms happen when powerful winds pick up sand and carry it over land.

trail (TRALE)
A rough pathway, usually in a wild area such as a desert or forest, used by hikers, cyclists, or horse riders.

Index

Read More

Owen, Ruth. *Roughing It
(DIY For Boys)*. New York:
Rosen Publishing (2014).

Rice, William B. *Death Valley
Desert (Time For Kids)*.
Huntington Beach, CA: Teacher
Created Materials (2012).

Learn More Online

To learn more about desert survival, go to
www.rubytuesdaybooks.com/desert